On the BeaTen PaTh
BEGINNING DRUMSET COURSE
n Inspiring Method to Playing the Drums, Guided by the Legends

LEVEL 3

AF271007

RICH LACKOWSKI

ALFRED

Alfred Music Publishing Co., Inc.
P.O. Box 10003
Van Nuys, CA 91410-0003
alfred.com

ISBN-10: 0-7390-7130-0
ISBN-13: 978-0-7390-7130-4

Cover Photos: Drumsets © Larry Lytle • Drumset provided courtesy of DW/PDP
Other photos: Vinnie Colaiuta Courtesy of The Avedis Zildjian Company, Inc. • Sly Dunbar © Wonder Knack
• Jon Fishman © Phish/Danny Clinch • Zigaboo Modeliste Courtesy of Vic Firth, Inc. • Neil Peart © Andrew MacNaughtan
• Jabo Starks Courtesy of Vic Firth, Inc. • Lars Ulrich © Neil Zlozower

 Alfred Cares. Contents printed on 100% recycled paper.

CONTENTS

CD audio examples performed by Rich Lackowski.
Instructional photos by Larry Lytle.

This book picks up where *On the Beaten Path: Beginning Drumset Course, Level 2* leaves off. It is designed to help you get "on the beaten path," that is, to help you play the beats and solos that our mighty drumming predecessors play on the songs we love. You will learn everything you need to know to go from the first thought of "I want to play the drums" to playing some of the most legendary beats and solos ever recorded! Many books claim to do this very thing, but what sets this book apart from the rest is that here, you will learn by playing along with the greatest drummers in the world—all types of famous drummers from a variety of musical styles—and you'll learn how to play the beats that they perform on some of the most famous songs ever recorded. This book explains what these drummers play on their songs by breaking it down in a way that gets you to learn to read music and start developing your own ideas into beats, fills, and solos.

I believe that drummers learn by mimicking their heroes. Sure, beats grow and change and morph into original ideas, but all drummers—from aspiring beginners to seasoned professionals—are naturally inspired by what other drummers are playing. The proof is in all those people you've seen air drumming along to some key part in a song. Many of these people have never sat behind a drumset or even held a drumstick, but the drum beat and the framework of the song somehow gets them to raise their arms in the air and act out their interpretation of a moving drum passage. It's

basic human instinct. When writing this book, I wanted to guide this natural instinct in a way that logically feeds you information as you need it so you can accelerate the process of learning how to play your drumming heroes' beats.

I know when I first started playing the drums, even though I had just begun taking group lessons on the snare drum in school, that the *real* learning happened when I got home and threw down my boring class snare drum book that our teacher assigned to us. I put on the headphones each day, sat behind my drum kit, and tried to mimic the beats and fills that the drummers were playing on my favorite songs. Through trial and error, I was eventually able to play the songs and at least fake my way through the more difficult parts.

In this book, I will accelerate this process of trial and error, and guide you through the things that every drummer needs to know in order to play the drums. This book can be used with or without a teacher. Although you don't *need* a teacher to use this book, it would benefit you to go find a drum teacher in your area and take lessons. A teacher will get you to practice if nothing else, but they will also correct any bad techniques you may be developing before they become hard-to-break habits.

Now let's get started and begin our journey On the Beaten Path!

Icons Used in This Book

The following icons are used throughout this book to help you learn valuable information and to become a better drummer.

TOOL: This icon is shown near key concepts or tools that will help you play the drums with more expression and personality.

TERM: This icon is shown near explanations of key music notations and concepts.

I'd like to thank everyone who helped bring this book to fruition. I am extremely grateful for each and every contribution, no matter how small, and your help is sincerely appreciated. Without your encouragement and support, this book would never have been possible.

I dedicate this book to my parents, Bob and Mary Jean, who helped me take the first steps down my drumming path. When I showed an interest in playing the drums, you were there to help me. When I needed a teacher, you hooked me up with one of the best around. And when I needed some encouragement, you were there supporting me every step of the way. Thank you for your patience as you listened to me fumble through the first several years of rushed fills, the repetitive beats that I played a zillion times, and my shortcomings when I didn't have even a faint concept of what it meant to groove. You helped empower what became a life-long passion and I thank you from the bottom of my heart for giving me that opportunity.

I also dedicate this book to my sisters, Janet and Chris; and my brothers-in-law, Sam and Scott, who each encouraged me to write my own path regardless of how difficult it may have been at times; and to the love of my life, my wonderful wife Nikki Lackowski, a constant source of love and encouragement, and an amazing woman who never stops believing in me or my talents.

Thanks to my friends and everyone that I've ever had the privilege of making music with, including Nikki O'Neill, Josh "Cartier" Cutsinger, Jon Sfondilis, Matt Hannon, Chris Moseman, Matt Lapperre, Tish Ciravolo, Ron Manus, Tommy Norton, Harold Branch, Jedd Scher, Cale Reese, Mark Ruppe, Paul Stabler, Todd Janko, and so many others who have embarked on various musical journeys with me. And thanks to every drummer mentioned in this book, and countless others who have inspired me to pick up the sticks and play the greatest instrument in the world.

A very special thanks to Ron Manus, a dear friend and a fun mentor; John O'Reilly Jr., Link Harnsberger, Holly Fraser, Mark Burgess, Kate Westin, Ted Engelbart, Glyn Dryhurst, Dave Black, Gwen Bailey-Harbour, Antonio Ferranti, Mike Finkelstein, Daniel Frohnen, Samantha Ordoñez, Ann Miranda, and the entire team at Alfred Music Publishing; Neil Larrivee and Mark Wessels at Vic Firth; Steve Lobmeier, Trish Johnson, Jim Bailey, Michael Robinson and all the wonderful people at Evans Drumheads; Don Lombardi, Juels Thomas, and Scott Donnell at DW Drums; John DeChristopher and Sarah Malaney at Zildjian; Frank Corniola and all the wonderful people at *Drumscene*; all the great folks at *Modern Drummer*; Phil Hood, Andy Doerschuk, and the folks at *DRUM!*; everyone at *Drumhead*, *Drummer*, *Rhythm*, and *Percussioni* magazines; Bernhard Castiglioni at Drummerworld.com; Mike Dolbear at MikeDolbear.com; Tiger Bill Meligari at TigerBill.com; Bart Elliott at DrummerCafe.com; Martin Osborne at Onlinedrummer.com; John Coia at Drum.com; Bob Gatzen; all the readers of *Modern Drummer* magazine and the readers of *DRUM!* magazine who voted for *On the Beaten Path: The Drummer's Guide to Musical Styles and the Legends Who Defined Them* as the "No. 1 Educational Book" in both of their 2008 Reader's Polls and who voted for *On the Beaten Path: Progressive Rock* among the winners in both of their 2009 Reader's Polls; and to Dean Turner, my first drum teacher who led me on my first steps down the beaten path. I thank you all from the bottom of my heart.

—Rich Lackowski

If you have completed *On the Beaten Path: Beginning Drumset Course, Level 1* and *On the Beaten Path: Beginning Drumset Course, Level 2,* you know the following things about playing the drums:

The Basics

Parts of a drumset, setting up the drums, holding the drumsticks, basic hand technique, basic foot technique, parts of a drum, tuning the drums, drumhead selection, drumstick selection, playing basic rock beats and fills, playing basic blues and shuffle beats and fills, double-stroke (open) rolls, multiple bounce (press/buzz) rolls, the 9-stroke roll, flams, drags, accents, ghost notes, rim clicks, crescendos, decrescendos, plus concepts including call and response, reading and playing cues, and improvisation.

Measures

Music notes are shown on a group of lines and spaces called a *staff*, which is divided into sections called *measures*.

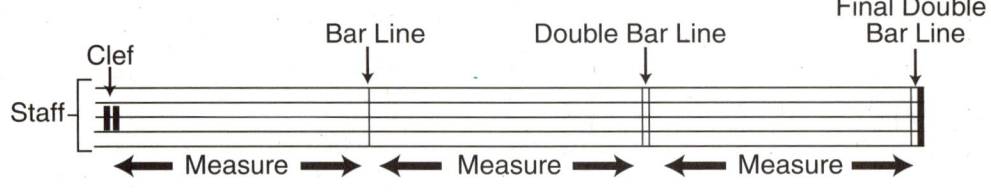

Bar lines indicate where measures begin and end. *Double bar lines* indicate a section break, like moving from a verse to a chorus in a song. *Final double bar lines* indicate the end of a piece.

At the beginning of each staff of music, there is a *clef sign*, which indicates how the music should be read. Unpitched percussion music typically uses the *neutral clef* (**II**).

A *repeat sign* has two dots before a final double bar line (:|) and indicates going back to the opposite-facing repeat sign (|:). If no opposite-facing repeat sign is present, repeat from the beginning of the music.

Notes and Rests

The duration of musical sounds (how long or short they are) is indicated by using different types of *notes*. Corresponding symbols called *rests* are used to indicate silence.
Notes are used to indicate musical sounds. Some notes are long and others are short.

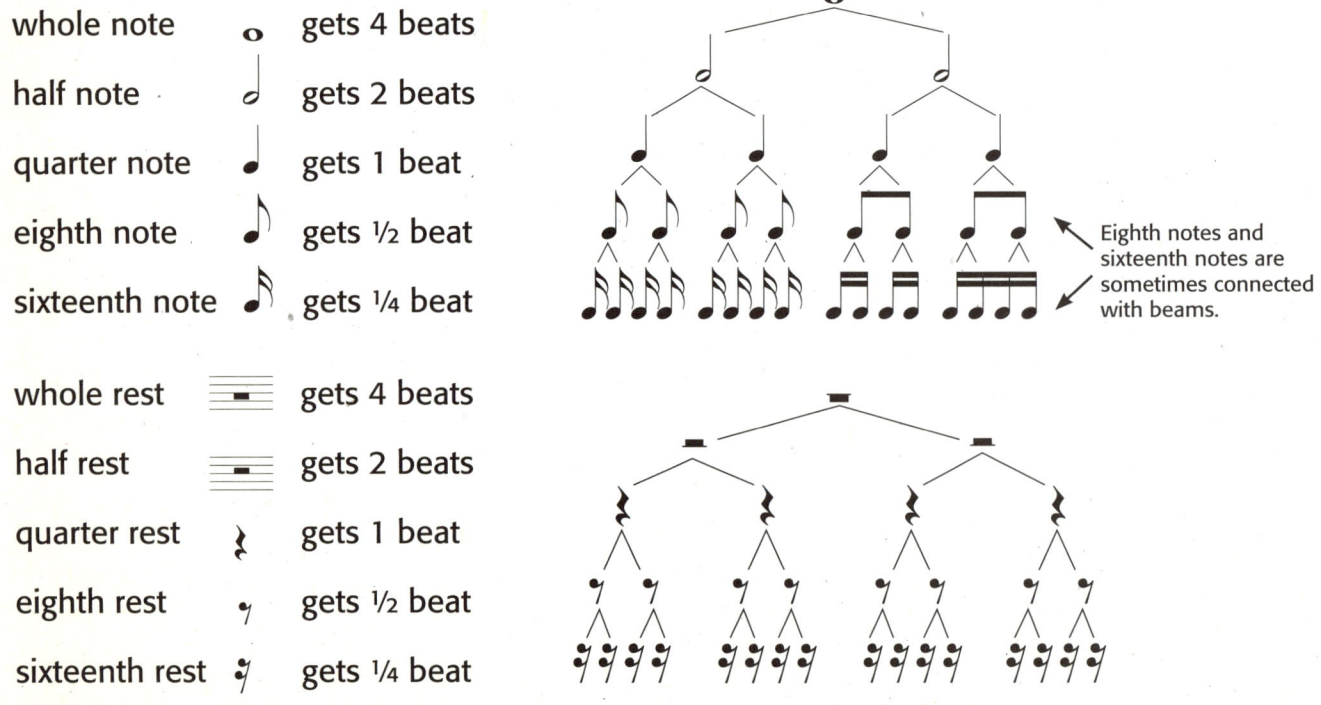

whole note   o   gets 4 beats

half note   𝅗𝅥   gets 2 beats

quarter note   ♩   gets 1 beat

eighth note   ♪   gets ½ beat

sixteenth note   𝅘𝅥𝅯   gets ¼ beat

Eighth notes and sixteenth notes are sometimes connected with beams.

whole rest   gets 4 beats

half rest   gets 2 beats

quarter rest   𝄽   gets 1 beat

eighth rest   𝄾   gets ½ beat

sixteenth rest   𝄿   gets ¼ beat

When a dot follows a note, the length of the note is longer by one half of the note's original length.

dotted half note   𝅗𝅥.   gets 3 beats

dotted quarter note   ♩.   gets 1 ½ beats

dotted eighth note   ♪.   gets ¾ beat

A triplet is a group of three notes played in the time of two notes of the same value. Triplets are identified by a small numeral 3 over the note group.

tri-ple-let
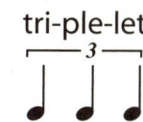

Time Signatures

A *time signature*, a symbol with two numbers, is placed at the beginning of a piece of music to indicate how the music is counted:
4 The top number shows the number of *beats* (or *counts*) in each measure, in this case, four.
4 The bottom number shows what kind of note gets one beat, in this case, a quarter note (♩).

In $\frac{4}{4}$ time, a whole note receives four beats.

A half note receives two beats.

A quarter note receives one beat.

An eighth note receives half of a beat.

A sixteenth note receives a quarter of a beat.

You will encounter other time signatures as well, which follow the same rules. For example, $\frac{12}{8}$ indicates that there are 12 beats per measure, with an eighth note getting one beat.

Tempo

Tempo is the speed of a musical piece or passage. Tempo is indicated by a musical term or by an exact *metronome marking*. A *metronome* is a device that clicks or flashes lights to indicate the tempo. For example, ♩ = 120 means the metronome will click 120 times per minute, and each click represents a quarter note.

Drum Notation

Each line and space of the staff designates a particular drum or cymbal.

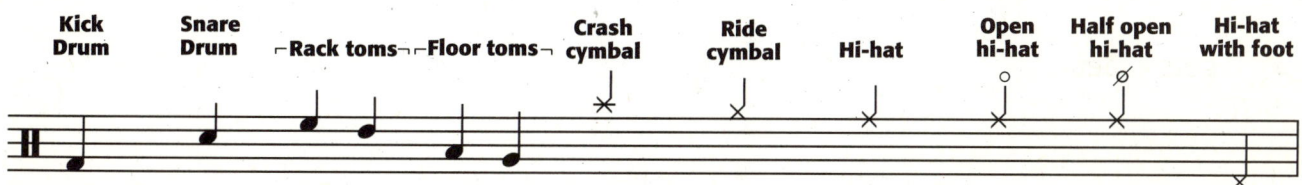

"On the Road Again"
FROM WILLIE NELSON'S *16 BIGGEST HITS* (1998, ORIGINALLY RELEASED ON THE *HONEYSUCKLE ROSE* SOUNDTRACK IN 1980)

"On the Road Again" is one of the most popular country songs of all time. Drummer Paul English, who has played with Nelson since 1955, lays down a standard country "train beat" by playing an accented two-handed pattern on the snare and playing the kick drum on beats 1 and 3.

Original transcription (0:25):

Let's start by playing the standard train beat. This groove is slightly swung, which means it's not played with ultra-precise eighth notes, and it's also not quite swung like a swing beat. Instead, it falls some-where in the middle of these two extremes. Play the kick on beats 1 and 3 while playing continuous eighth notes on the snare, alternating left and right hands. Be sure to accent beats 2 and 4. Go ahead and give it a try.

Sometimes drummers add an extra eighth note in the train beat, just to give it a slight variation, which keeps it interesting.

Another common variation in the train beat is adding an additional accent to the "&" of beat 1 or, in this exercise, to the "&" of beat 3.

First and second endings

First and second endings are used in music notation when a section of music is played the same all the way through except for the ending. Instead of writing the music out twice with only the ending of the section changing, the use of first and second endings make it easier to notate and easier for the musician to read.

"The Devil Went Down to Georgia"
FROM THE CHARLIE DANIELS BAND'S *MILLION MILE REFLECTIONS* (1979)

Similar in feel to "On the Road Again" but much faster, this is a good example of a *train beat*, competently played by drummer James Marshall. This lesson features an eight bar excerpt and is notated using first and second endings. When you get to the repeat sign (first ending), go back to the opposite facing repeat sign which, in this case, is at the beginning of the transcription. When you finish playing the third measure the second time, skip the first ending and jump straight to the second ending, which adds an accent on the "&" of beat 3. Go ahead and give it a try!

Track 4

Original transcription (0:21):

BASIC FUNK BEATS

"Groovy Lady"
FROM THE METERS' *FUNKIFY YOUR LIFE: THE METERS ANTHOLOGY* (1995)

Joseph "Zigaboo" Modeliste is one of the funkiest drummers on the planet. If you would like to play funk music, do yourself a favor and buy this album. It's loaded with some of the best funk drumming ever played, as demonstrated in this excerpt from "Groovy Lady."

Original transcription (Intro):

Track 5

Let's start by playing sixteenth notes on the hi-hat by alternating each stick, starting with your right hand. Hit the snare on beats 2 and 4 with your right hand. Play the kick on beats 1 and 3, on the "&" of beats 2 and 4, and on the "ah" of beats 1 and 3.

Now, add in the accents on beats 1 and 3, and the additional kick drum hits on beats 2 and 4 and you'll be playing the funky beat just like Zigaboo plays it on the recording!

"Doodle Loop (The World is a Little Bit Under the Weather)"
FROM THE METERS' *FUNKIFY YOUR LIFE: THE METERS ANTHOLOGY* (1995)

This tune also features some funky playing by Zigaboo Modeliste and showcases some of his beautifully syncopated kick drum playing.

Original transcription (Intro):

Track 6

Let's start by playing eighth notes on the hi-hat, the snare on beats 2 and 4, and the kick drum on beats 1 and 3, and on the "&" of beats 2 and 4.

Now, let's play the same groove as in the previous lesson, only this time, we'll add kick drum hits on the "ah" of beats 1 and 3.

Finally, play the same groove as in the previous lesson, but this time, remove the kick drum hit on beat 3. Start slowly and gradually increase the tempo as you feel comfortable.

ZIGABOO MODELISTE

Widely acknowledged as the innovator of second-line funk playing, Zigaboo Modeliste is without a doubt one of the most influential, creative, and soulful artists to ever live. This highly acclaimed drummer and New Orleans legend has written and recorded over 200 songs with The Meters, spanning 30 national and international album releases. He's touched many with his incredible playing and will forever be considered the king of funk drumming.

"Unfunky UFO"
FROM PARLIAMENT'S *MOTHERSHIP CONNECTION* (1976)

This album is widely accepted as Parliament's best, and is definitely one of the "must-hear" milestones on the beaten path of funk. Parliament was notorious for having a revolving door of members throughout their long career, and four drummers are credited on this album, including bassist Bootsy Collins. So it's a bit unclear as to which drummer played on which songs, but all the drummers—Jerome "Bigfoot" Brailey, Bootsy Collins, Gary "Mudbone" Cooper, and Ramon Tiki Fulwood—are incredibly talented, unbelievably funky, and worth checking out.

Original transcription (0:22):

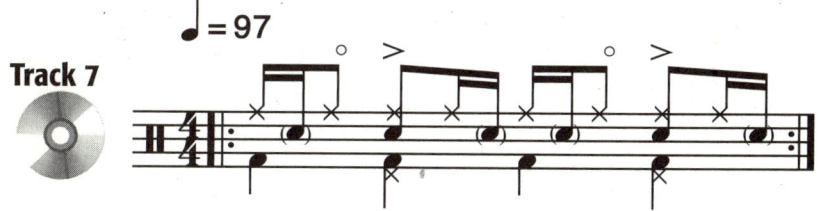

Let's start by playing a simple "four on the floor" beat.

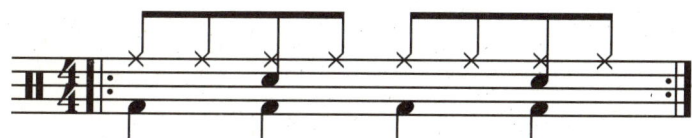

Now, let's add a ghost note on the snare on the "ah" of beats 2 and 4. Pay careful attention to playing the ghost notes at a much quieter volume then the accented snare hits on beats 2 and 4.

Next, let's play the "four on the floor" beat, and this time, let's play a ghost note on the "e" of beats 1 and 3. Again, make sure there is a large contrast in volume between the ghost notes and the accented notes.

Now, let's combine the previous two exercises and play the "four on the floor" beat with accented snare hits on beats 2 and 4, and ghost notes on the "e" of beats 1 and 3, and on the "ah" of beats 2 and 4.

Next, let's play the same beat as in the previous exercise, but this time, let's play it with an open hi-hat on the "&" of each beat by stomping your left foot on the hi-hat pedal on beats 1, 2, 3, and 4.

Finally, let's play the same beat as in the previous exercise, but this time, we'll remove the open hi-hat hits on the "&" of beats 2 and 4 by only stomping your foot on the hi-hat pedal on beats 2 and 4.

"You Can Make It If You Try"
FROM SLY & THE FAMILY STONES' *STAND!* (1969)

Drummer Greg Errico lays down quite a driving funk groove starting at 0:52 into this song. He achieves this driving feel by playing the snare drum on beats 1, 2, and 4, and by playing a syncopated kick drum pattern.

Original transcription (0:52):

Track 8

Let's start by playing eighth notes on the hi-hat, the snare on beats 1, 2 and 4, and the kick drum on beat 3 and on the "&" of beat 3.

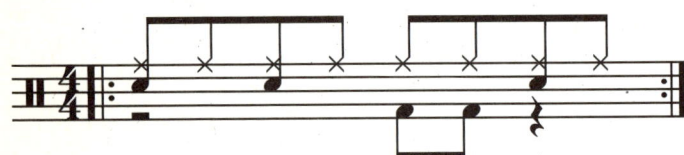

Now, let's add in some additional kick drum hits. You may need to practice this slowly at first and gradually increase the tempo as you feel comfortable.

Finally, add in the last kick drum hit on the "e" of beat 1, and you'll be playing the groove just like Greg Errico plays it on the original recording!

"Tippi-Toes"
FROM THE METERS' *STRUTTIN'* (1970)

Zigaboo incorporates syncopated kick drum hits and open hi-hat hits into this gloriously funky groove.

Original transcription (0:19):

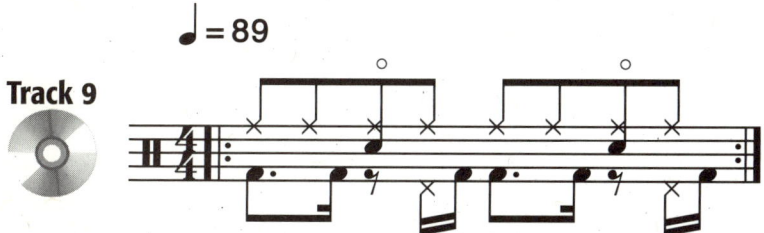

Track 9

Let's start by playing eighth notes on the hi-hat, the snare on beats 2 and 4, and the kick drum on beats 1 and 3. Lift your left foot off the hi-hat pedal on beats 2 and 4, and stomp your foot back down on the pedal on the "&" of beats 2 and 4.

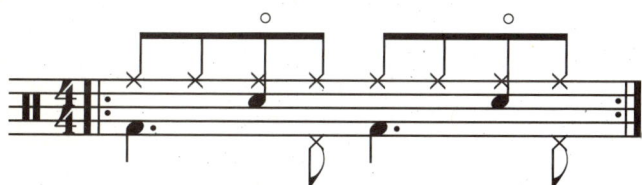

Next, let's play the same groove as in the previous lesson, but this time, we'll add kick drum hits on the "ah" of beats 1 and 3.

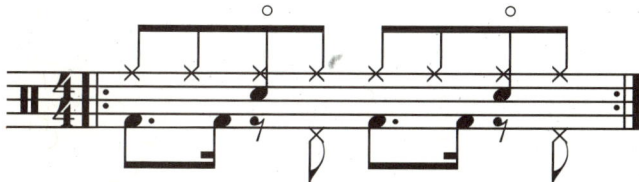

Finally, add kick drum hits on the "ah" of beats 2 and 4 and you'll be playing this ultra funky groove just like Zigaboo plays it on the recording!

"Brick House"
FROM THE COMMODORES' *COMMODORES* (1977)

This is definitely one of the most popular and widely-covered funk tunes ever written. Drummer Walter Orange plays this contagious beat that's been heard by generations of dancers all around the world.

Original transcription (0:30):

Track 10

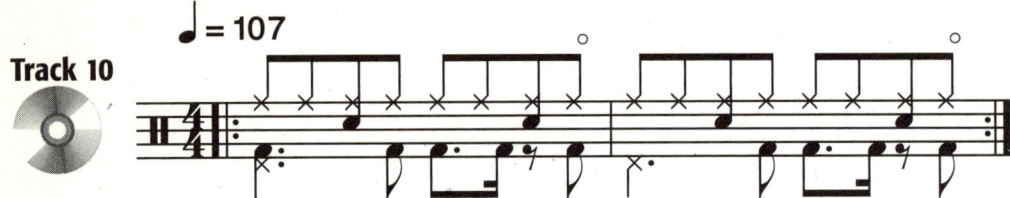

Let's start by playing this simplified version of the groove. Play eighth notes on the hi-hat, the snare on beats 2 and 4, and the kick on beats 1 and 3, and on the "&" of beats 2 and 4.

Now, let's spice up the beat by opening the hi-hat on the "&" of beat 4 and closing it again on beat 1 of the following measure.

Next, let's add an additional kick hit on the "ah" of beat 3.

Now, let's play the same groove as in the previous lesson, but this time, let's remove the kick drum hit that was played on beat 1.

Finally, put it all together and play the groove just like Walter Orange played it on the recording!

"Chameleon"
FROM HERBIE HANCOCK'S *HEAD HUNTERS* (1973)

Drummer Harvey Mason plays a seriously funky groove on this, one of the most popular funk tunes ever written.

Original transcription (0:16):

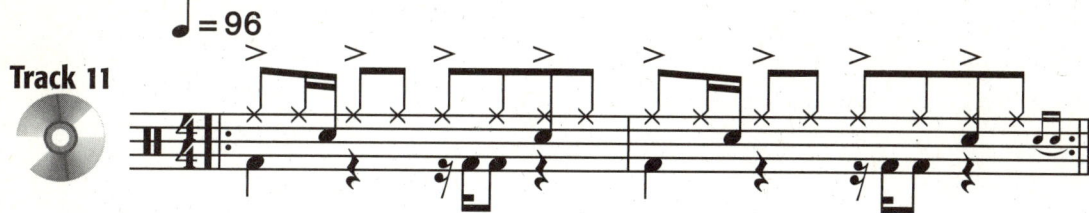

Let's start by playing eighth notes on the hi-hat, kick on beat 1 and on the "&" of beat 3, and the snare on the "ah" of beat 1 and on beat 4. Start slowly at first and gradually increase the tempo as you feel comfortable.

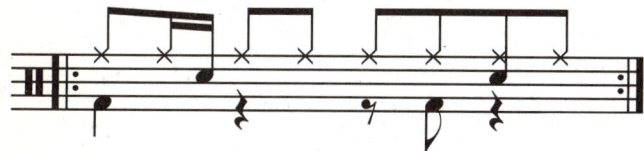

Now, let's play the same groove as in the previous lesson, but this time, we'll add a kick hit on the "e" of beat 3. Go ahead and give it a try.

Next, let's play the same groove as in the previous exercise, but this time, we'll add a drag on the snare drum that leads into the kick drum and hi-hat hits on beat 1 of the following measure. Go ahead and give it a try.

Now, put it all together, add accents on the hi-hat on beats 1, 2, 3, and 4, and you'll be playing the funky groove just like Harvey Mason plays it on the recording!

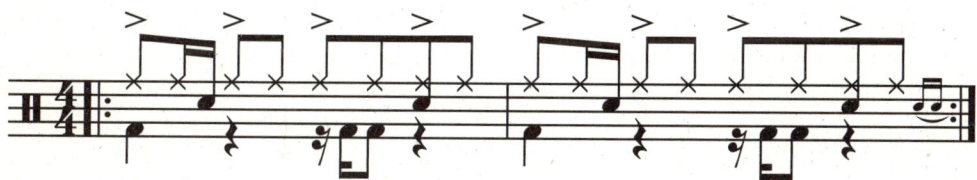

"Thinking"
FROM THE METERS' *LOOK-KA PY PY* (1969)

This is another example of Zigaboo's incredibly funky drumming. One thing that makes this beat so fun to play is that the open hi-hat, which begins on beat 4, only lasts for half of one beat. You'll start to hear this concept quite a bit as you listen to more and more funk music.

Original transcription (0:01):

Track 12

Let's start by playing quarter notes on the hi-hat, the snare on beats 2 and 4, and the kick drum on beat 1, and on the "&" and "ah" of beat 3.

Next, let's play the same groove as in the previous exercise, but this time we'll add an open hi-hat on beat 4. For this exercise, let's let that open hi-hat ring out all the way until beat 1 of the following measure, at which point you'll stomp your foot back on the hi-hat pedal. Go ahead and give it a try!

Finally, let's play the same beat, but this time we'll shorten the duration of the open hi-hat that starts on beat 4 to last the duration of an eighth note. To do this, lift your foot off the hi-hat pedal on beat 4, and stomp your foot back down on the pedal on the "&" of beat 4. Practice this slowly and be patient. You can do it!

James Brown, after much persistence, convinced Jabo Starks to leave his gig with the Bobby "Blue" Band and join the James Brown Orchestra in 1965. Jabo recorded the drums on more charting singles than any other drummer in James Brown's extensive career, including "Sex Machine," "Papa Don't Take No Mess," "Make It Funky," "Super Bad," "The Payback," "Doin' It to Death," and "Licking Stick," just to name a few.

"Super Bad, Pt. 1"
FROM JAMES BROWN'S *70'S FUNK CLASSICS* (2004, SINGLE ORIGINALLY RELEASED IN 1970)

John "Jabo" Starks plays one of the all-time greatest and funkiest beats ever recorded on this tune. Listen to how Jabo skillfully incorporates his trademark open hi-hat hits on the "&" of beats 1 and 3 while he plays syncopated snare hits and a steady kick drum pattern that glues it all together. Now that's some funky drumming!

Original transcription (0:02):

♩ = 126

Track 13

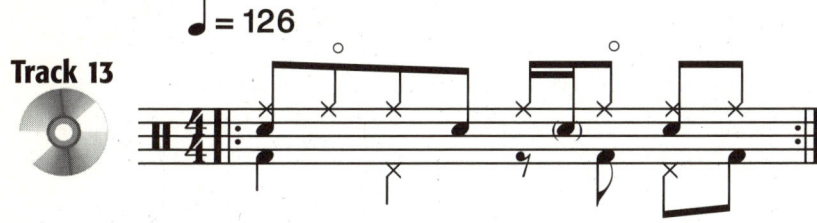

Let's begin by playing eighth notes on the hi-hat, and add in the syncopated snare hits on beat 1, the "&" of beat 2, and on beat 4.

Next, let's add in kick drum hits on beat 1 and the "&" of beats 3 and 4.

Now, add a ghosted snare hit on the "e" of beat 3.

Next, open the hi-hat on the "&" of beat 1 and close it again on beat 2.

Finally, add an additional open hi-hat on the "&" of beat 3 and you'll be playing this super funky beat just like Jabo plays it on the recording.

"54-46 That's My Number"
FROM TOOTS & THE MAYTALS' *THE VERY BEST OF TOOTS & THE MAYTALS* (2000, SINGLE ORIGINALLY RELEASED IN 1968)

Drummer Paul Douglas plays a classic one-drop beat on this tune by one of the pioneering bands of reggae music. Play quarter notes on the hi-hat on beats 1, 2, 3 and 4, while playing a rim click and a simultaneous kick drum hit on beat 3. Go ahead and give it a try!

Original transcription (0:04):

One-Drop

The one-drop rhythm is a groove that dominates roots reggae drumming with the kick drum landing on beat 3, or, depending on how the song is counted and notated, on beats 2 and 4 of each measure. The groove got its name from the intentional omission of beat 1 on the kick drum. The "one" is dropped in this popular reggae rhythm.

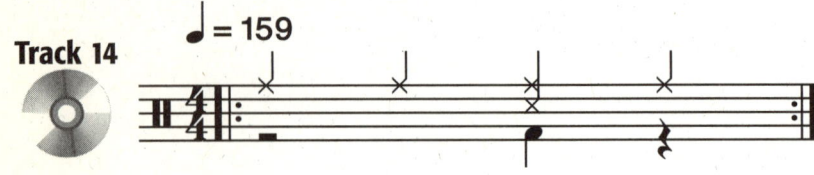

"Buffalo Soldier"
FROM BOB MARLEY AND THE WAILERS' *CONFRONTATION* (1983)

Carlton Barrett plays another type of reggae beat in this tune where the kick is played on beats 1, 2, 3, and 4, and a rim click is played on beat 3 of the first two measures, and on the last note of the triplet that starts on beat 4 in the second measure.

Original transcription (0:24):

One-Measure Repeat

One-measure repeats are used to indicate that you should play exactly what was written in the previous measure. When notated, a one-measure repeat looks like this:

"One Love / People Get Ready"
FROM BOB MARLEY AND THE WAILERS' *EXODUS* (1977)

Carlton Barrett masterfully incorporates accented notes and a bouncy hi-hat feel on this timeless tune.

Track 16

Original transcription (0:02):

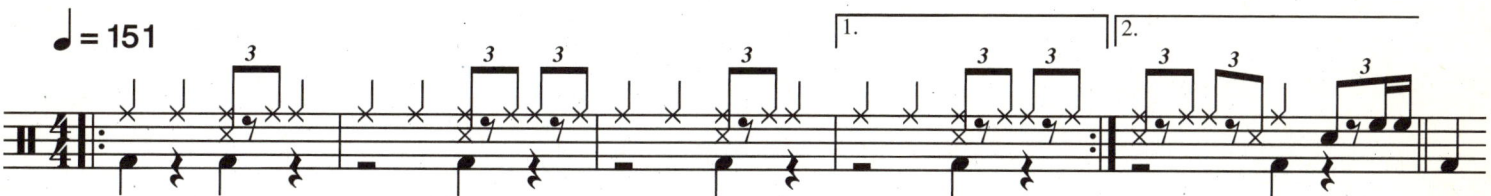

Let's start by playing and repeating a basic one-drop rhythm by hitting the hi-hat on beats 1, 2, 3, and 4, and playing a rim click and a kick drum hit together on beat 3.

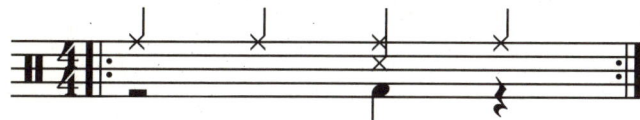

Sometimes, reggae drummers embellish the beat a bit by varying the hits on the hi-hat. The bouncy feel that they achieve is similar to what we learned when playing a swing beat. Start slowly and gradually increase the tempo as you feel comfortable.

In this next exercise, we'll play a very common reggae drum fill followed by a simple one-drop rhythm. To play the fill, hit a rim click on beat 1 and on the last note of the triplet that starts on beat 2. Then, hit the snare on beat 4 with the snares turned off so it sounds like a high-pitched rack tom or a timbale.

Finally, let's put it all together, adding the rack tom to the fill, and play this one-drop reggae groove just like Carlton Barrett plays it on the recording!

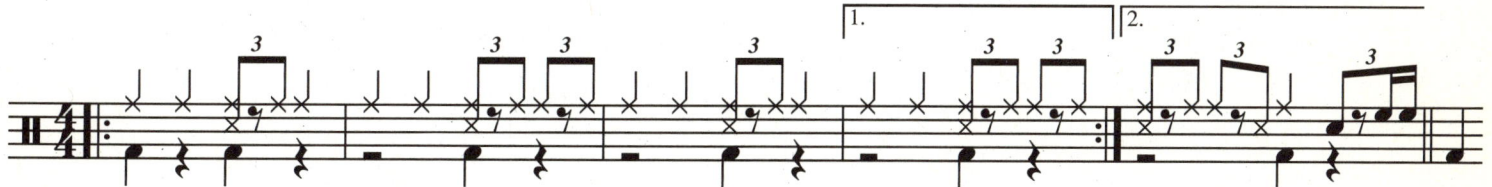

"Rootsman Skanking"

FROM BUNNY WAILERS' *ROOTSMAN SKANKING* (1987)

Sly Dunbar, one of the most prolific and important drummers to ever come out of Jamaica, plays this fantastic reggae beat that mixes rim clicks, snare hits, and open hi-hats together to create a groove that perfectly compliments this song.

Original transcription (0:01):

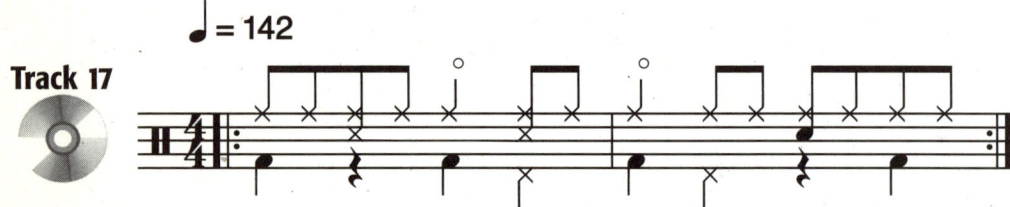

Let's start by playing this simplified version of the groove.

Next, let's play the same beat as in the last exercise, but this time, we'll open the hi-hat on beat 3 of the first measure, and on beat 1 of the second measure.

Now, let's play eighth notes on the hi-hat in the first measure whenever you're not playing an open hi-hat. When you are playing an open hi-hat, let the cymbals ring out for a full quarter note beat.

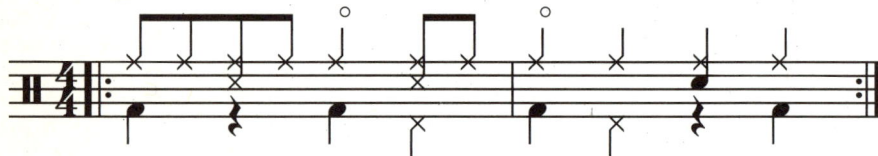

Finally, play eighth notes on the hi-hat in the second measure when you're not playing an open hi-hat. Start slowly and increase the tempo as you feel comfortable.

Dunbar taught himself to play the drums at age 15 by listening to and mimicking his earliest influencers, Carlton Barrett (The Wailers) and Lloyd Knibb (The Skatalites). Throughout his over-30-year career playing the drums and producing music, Sly Dunbar has revolutionized the Jamaican sound time and time again. He will forever be regarded as one of the most innovative musicians associated with the reggae genre and all of its derivatives.

BASIC LATIN BEATS

"The Girl from Ipanema"
FROM ASTRUD GILBERTO, JOÃO GILBERTO, & STAN GETZ'S GETZ/GILBERTO (1964)

This is quite possibly the most popular bossa nova tune ever written. Drummer Milton Banana plays a very straight forward groove, primarily on the hi-hat, with a few accents added throughout. Go ahead and try playing along with the groove that's notated here.

Bossa Nova
The bossa nova rhythm is a common groove found in Brazilian music.

Original transcription (0:22):

Track 18

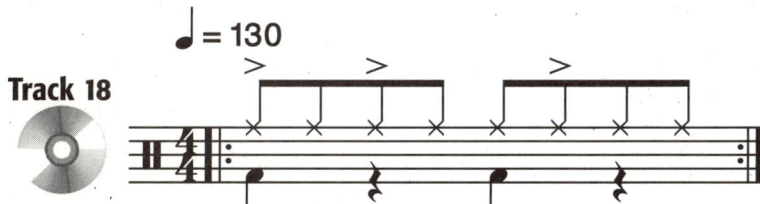

This next lesson shows a very common bossa nova groove. Go ahead and try playing this groove along with the tune. The rim clicks are very important, so make sure you pay special attention to hitting them in the right places.

Track 19

"Fee"
FROM PHISH'S *JUNTA* (1989)

The bossa nova beat has found its way into other styles of music. In this tune, drummer Jon Fishman adapts a bossa nova groove into a jam band setting.

Original transcription (0:15):

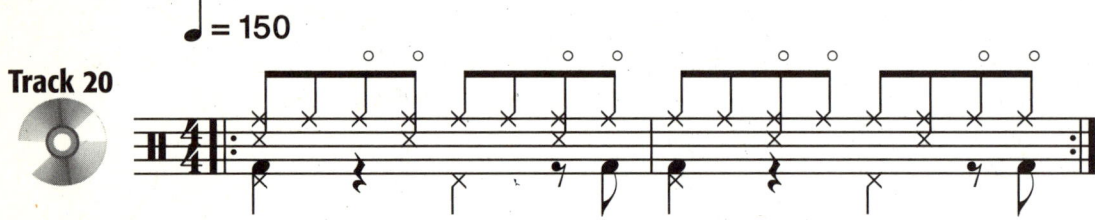

Let's start by playing eighth notes on the hi-hat with your right hand. Press the hi-hat pedal down with your left foot on beats 1 and 3, and raise your left foot off the pedal on beats 2 and 4.

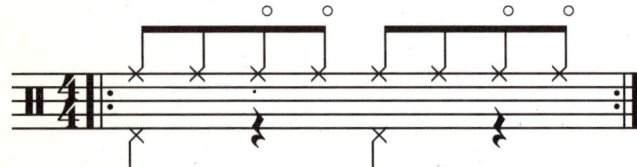

Now, play the same groove as in the previous lesson, but this time, add a rim click on beat 1, the "&" of beat 2, and on beat 4 in the first measure, and on beat 2 and the "&" of beat 3 in the second measure.

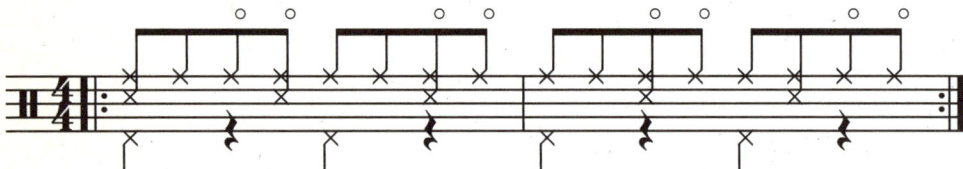

Next, let's play the same groove as in the previous lesson, but this time, let's add a kick drum hit on beat 1 of each measure.

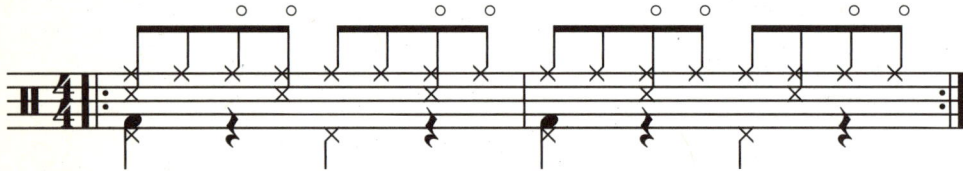

Finally, add another kick drum hit on the "&" of beat 4 in each measure, and you'll be playing the groove just like Jon Fishman plays it on the recording!

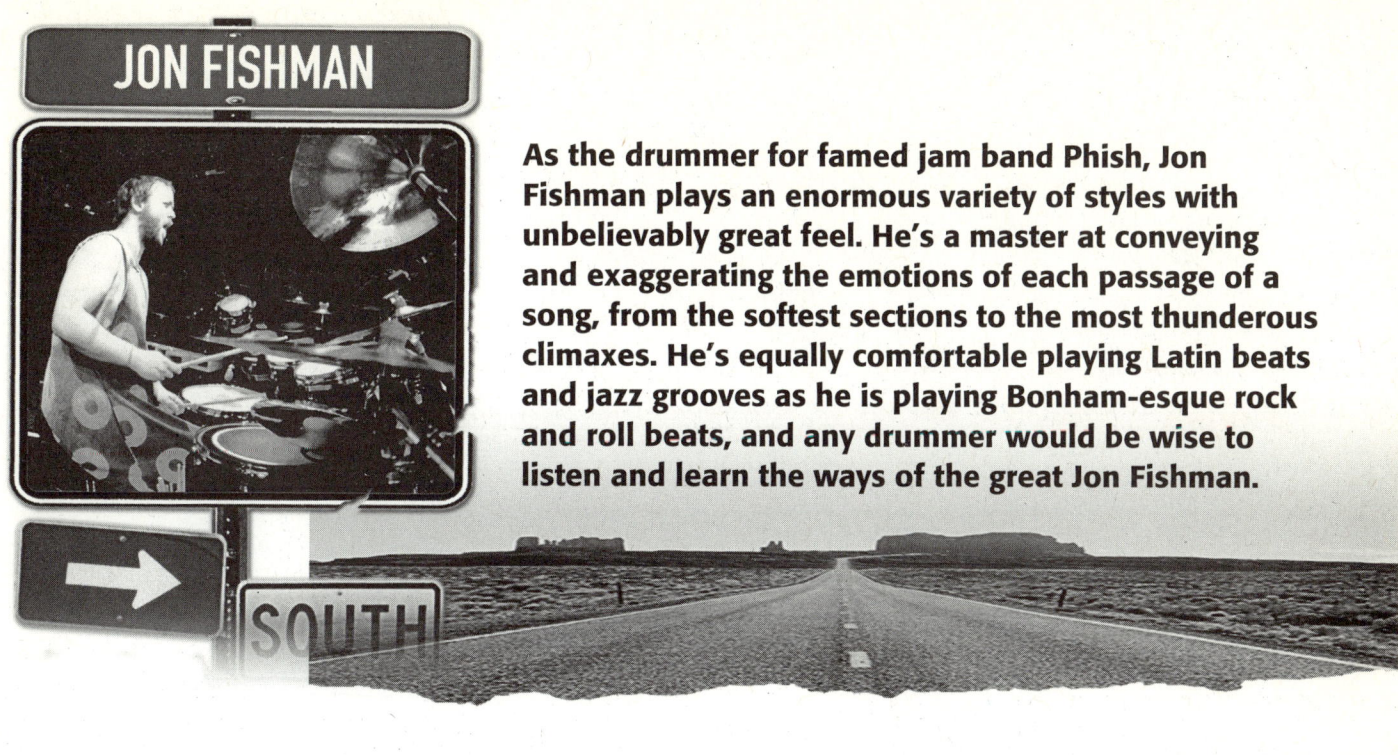

As the drummer for famed jam band Phish, Jon Fishman plays an enormous variety of styles with unbelievably great feel. He's a master at conveying and exaggerating the emotions of each passage of a song, from the softest sections to the most thunderous climaxes. He's equally comfortable playing Latin beats and jazz grooves as he is playing Bonham-esque rock and roll beats, and any drummer would be wise to listen and learn the ways of the great Jon Fishman.

"Desafinado (Off Key)"
FROM CHARLIE BYRD & STAND GETZ'S *JAZZ SAMBA* (1962)

Drummers Buddy Deppenschmidt and Bill Reichenbach play an up-tempo bosa nova groove in this famous tune. This transcription and lesson is a drumset adaptation of the original groove that blends together the drum and percussion parts played by Deppenschmidt and Reichenback. An interesting note is that drummer John Densmore took this basic bossa nova groove and played it at a blazing 188 BPM in the song "Break On Through (To the Other Side)" from the Doors's self-titled debut album.

Original transcription (0:14):

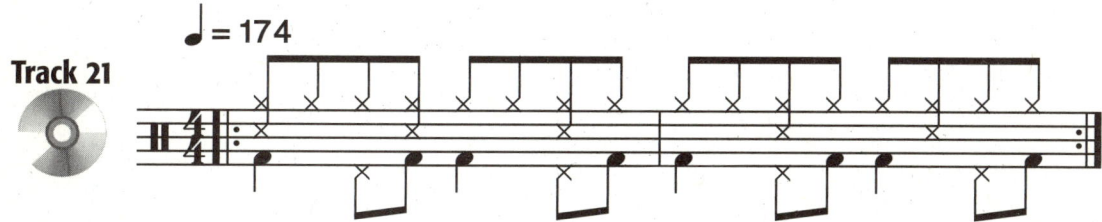

Let's start by playing eighth notes on the ride cymbal, the kick on beats 1 and 3, and on the "&" of beats 2 and 4, and the hi-hat with your foot on beats 2 and 4.

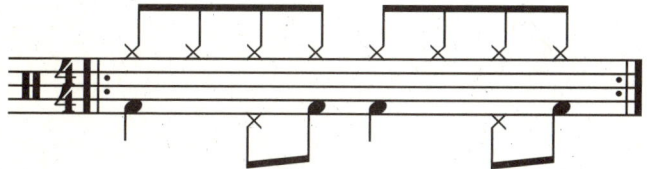

Next, let's play the same groove as in the previous lesson, but this time, we'll add rim clicks on beats 1 and 4 of the first measure, and to beat 2 of the second measure.

Finally, add in another rim click on the "&" of beat 2 in the first measure, and on the "&" of beat 3 in the second measure and you'll be playing the bossa nova groove! If you play it faster, at 188 BPM, you'll be playing the groove in "Break on Through (To the Other Side)!"

We learned dozens of jazz beats and fills in Level 2 of the *On the Beaten Path: Beginning Drumset Course*. Here, in the next two sections of this book, we continue our exploration of this great genre with more jazz beats and jazz fills to round out your drumming skills and to introduce new musical concepts. Enjoy!

Dropping Bombs

Dropping bombs is a term that refers to a drummer placing unexpected kick drum hits within a jazz groove. Dropping bombs is common in bebop-style drumming (a sub-genre of jazz usually characterized by very fast tempos and virtuoso musicians) and was pioneered by drummers Kenny Clarke, Max Roach, and Art Blakey.

"In Walked Bud"
FROM THELONIOUS MONK'S *THE VERY BEST* (2005, SONG ORIGINALLY RECORDED IN 1947)

Art Blakey masterfully plays some of his famous bomb drops on this jazz standard, composed by the great Thelonious Monk. This excerpt begins with some bomb drops in the first two measures, and then switches to some syncopated snare hits in the last two measures.

Track 22   Original transcription (0:24):

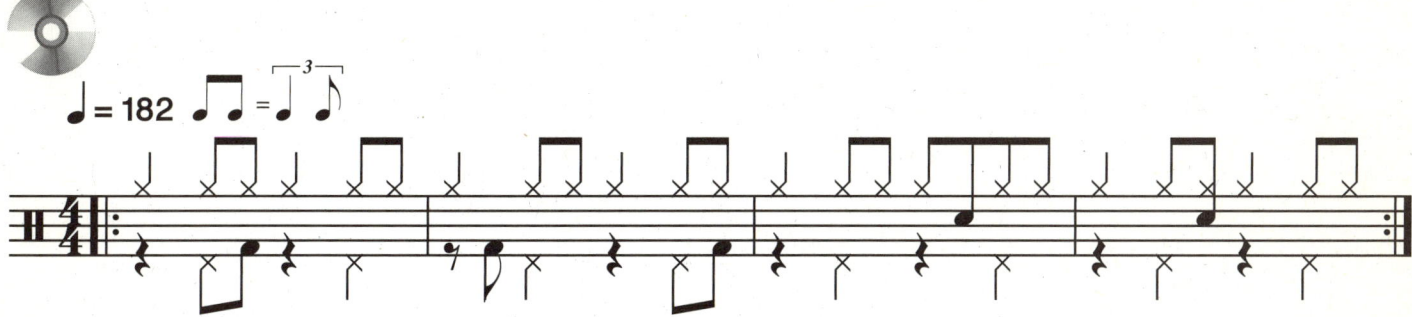

Let's begin by isolating and repeating the first measure of the excerpt. At a slow tempo, play a couple measures of the basic swing pattern on the ride cymbal with your right hand and the hi-hat with your foot. Then starting on measure 3 of this exercise, add in the bomb drop by playing the kick on the "&" of beat 2 and repeat that measure until you can play this comfortably. Gradually increase the tempo as you feel comfortable.

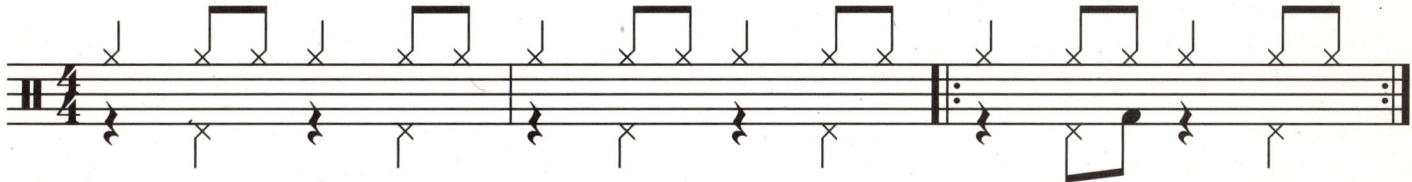

Now, let's isolate and repeat the second measure of the excerpt. This time, the bomb drops occur on the "&" of beats 1 and 4. Like in the previous lesson, we'll begin by playing a couple measures of the traditional swing pattern before proceeding to the bomb drops in measure 3. Go ahead and give it a try, slowly at first, and gradually faster as you feel comfortable.

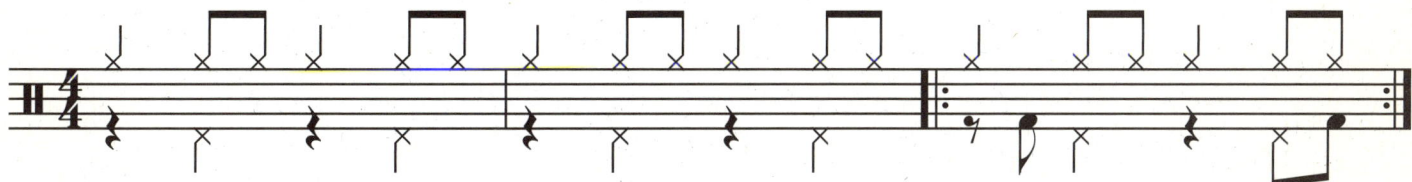

Let's combine what we learned in the previous two lessons and practice playing and repeating the first two measures of the excerpt. Again, we'll start with a couple measures of keeping time before incorporating the bomb drops.

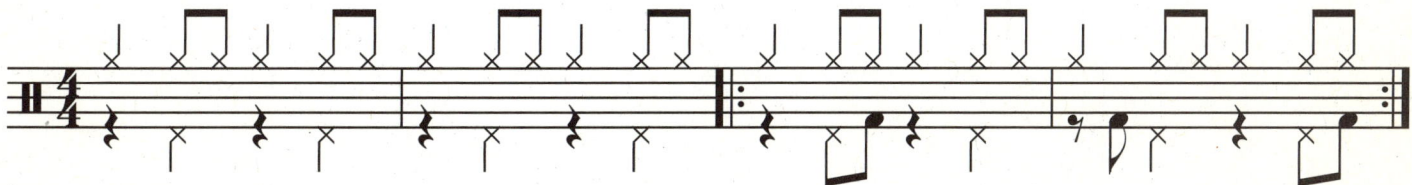

Next, let's isolate and repeat the last two measures of the excerpt. Begin by playing a basic swing pattern for two measures, and starting in measure 3, play the syncopated snare hits with your left hand on the "&" of beat 3, and the "&" of beat 2 in the fourth measure. Start slowly and increase the tempo as you feel comfortable.

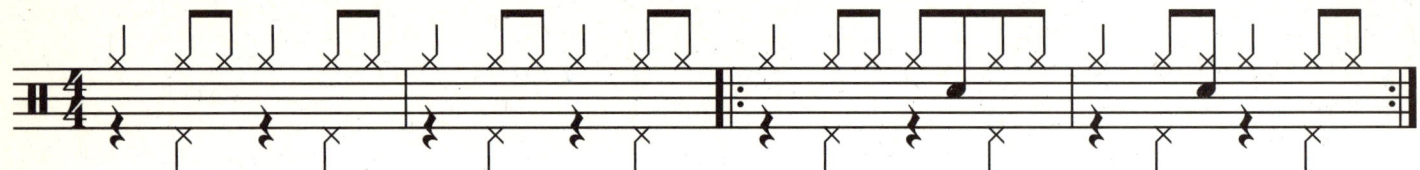

Finally, let's put it all together and play the excerpt complete with bomb drops and syncopated snare hits just like Art Blakey plays it on the recording.

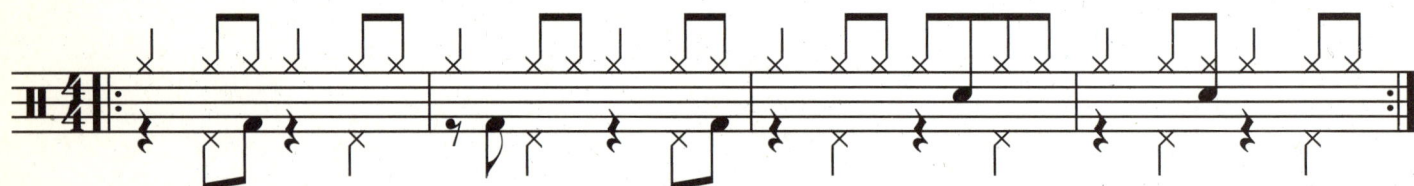

MORE JAZZ FILLS

"In Walked Bud" (ex. 1)
FROM THELONIOUS MONK'S *THE VERY BEST*
(2005, SONG ORIGINALLY RECORDED IN 1947)

Art Blakey plays some quick snare hits before ending the fill with a quarter-note triplet with his left hand on the snare while playing quarter notes on the ride with his right hand. The result is a "2 against 3" polyrhythm, with two beats played on the ride with the right hand for every three beats played on the snare with the left hand. Go ahead and give the fill a try. Start slowly at first, and gradually increase the speed as you feel comfortable.

Polyrhythms

A *polyrhythm* is a rhythm of one type played against a rhythm of a different type. A common example of a polyrhythm is when you play eighth notes on top of eighth note triplets. There are two eighth notes played for every three eighth notes in a triplet, so this is a "2 against 3" polyrhythm.

Original transcription (1:48):

Track 23

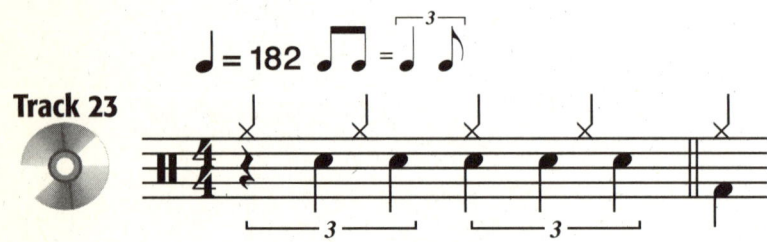

Now, let's practice playing the fill within the context of the beat.

Track 24

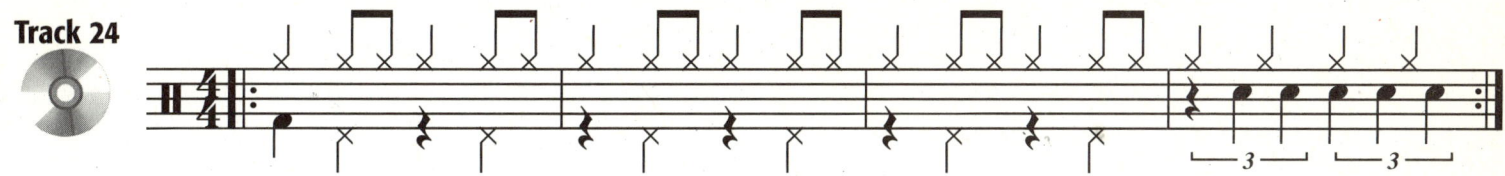

"In Walked Bud" (ex. 2)

FROM THELONIOUS MONK'S *THE VERY BEST* (2005, SONG ORIGINALLY RECORDED IN 1947)

Art Blakey plays a simple, yet elegant, fill in this excerpt with a smooth open roll that starts on beat 3 and continues until beat 1 of the following measure. Notice how smoothly Blakey plays this so the momentum of the groove never stops. Go ahead and give it a try.

Original transcription (0:44):

Track 25

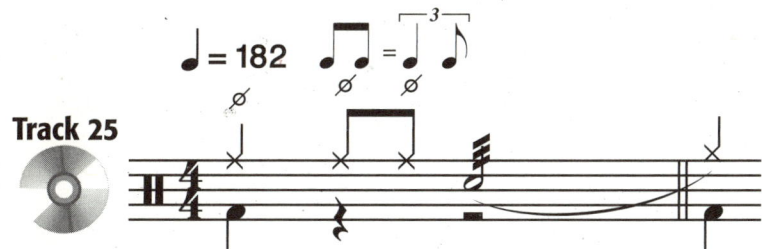

Now, let's practice playing the fill within the context of the beat.

Track 26

Rim Shot

A *rim shot* is played by hitting the tip of the stick on the head of the snare drum while simultaneously hitting the shaft of the stick on the rim of the drum. The resulting sound is a loud, accented, high-pitched, explosive crack.

"Straight, No Chaser"
FROM MILES DAVIS'S *MILESTONES* (1958)

It's clear why Miles Davis loved playing with "Philly" Joe Jones. Listen to how effortless, yet complex, Jones's playing is. "Philly" Joe had a gift to which we mortal drummers all aspire. This excerpt showcases some very tasty left hand snare work in the first measure, followed by a quick sixteenth-note fill starting on the "&" of beat 1 in the second measure that continues until slamming a rim shot down on beat 3, and finishing with some simultaneous ride and kick hits.

Original transcription (9:23):

Let's start by isolating and repeating the first measure of the fill. There are a lot of snare embellishments played with the left hand in this part of the fill, so start slowly, and gradually increase the tempo as you feel comfortable.

Now, let's play and repeat the following two-bar example. The first measure is fairly simple, and it sets up the simultaneous hit on the snare and the ride on the "&" of beat 4 so you are ready to play the second measure of the fill. At the end of the string of sixteenth notes played in the second measure, hit a nice, strong rim shot on beat 3 by hitting the tip of the stick on the drumhead while simultaneously hitting the shaft of the stick on the rim of the drum. This will take a little practice at first, but stick with it.

Finally, let's play the first measure of the two-bar fill with all the snare embellishments, continue on to the second measure with the sixteenth notes, rim shot, and simultaneous ride and kick hits, and with a little practice, you'll be playing the drum fill just like "Philly" Joe Jones plays it on the recording.

Open Hi-Hat Foot Splash

An *open hi-hat foot splash* is played by quickly bouncing the ball of the foot off the hi-hat pedal and raising the foot off of the pedal immediately after the cymbals have made contact with each other. The resulting sound is similar to playing a slightly open hi-hat with a drumstick and then letting the cymbals ring openly afterwards. When notated, an open hi-hat foot splash looks like this:

"So What"
FROM MILES DAVIS'S
KIND OF BLUE (1959)

Jimmy Cobb's legendary drum fill from the opening track of the most famous jazz recording of all-time stands among the best drumming moments in history. Cobb, playing with a stick in his left hand and a wire brush in his right, effortlessly combines the snare, toms, kick, and open/closed hi-hat to create a gorgeous fill that launches Miles and the band into jazz bliss. Notice how Cobb, in all his glory, switches the wire brush over to his left hand and the stick to over his right hand after he hits the crash at the conclusion of the drum fill. Very cool stuff!

Original transcription (1:29):

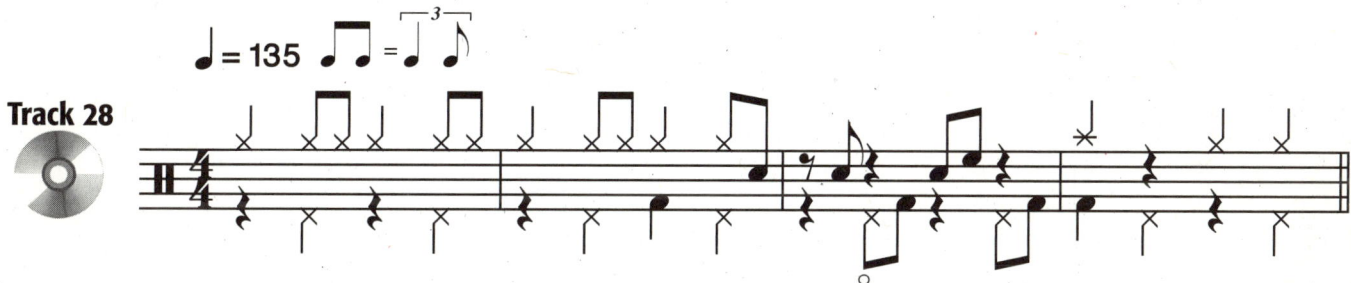

Track 28

Let's start by playing and repeating a simplified version of the fill. Begin by hitting the crash cymbal with the stick in your left hand, and continue by playing a swing pattern on the ride with the brush in your right hand. Hit the kick drum on beat 3, and hit the snare drum with your right brush on the "&" of beat 4. Continue the fill by playing another snare hit with the right brush on the "&" of beat 1 of the following measure, and then an open hi-hat splash with your left foot on beat 2. Creating this open hi-hat splash sound with your foot will take some effort, but with a little practice, you'll be playing it in no time. This lesson concludes with another snare hit on beat 3 followed by a hi-hat hit with your left foot on beat 4, and then the whole exercise repeats. Go ahead and give it a try.

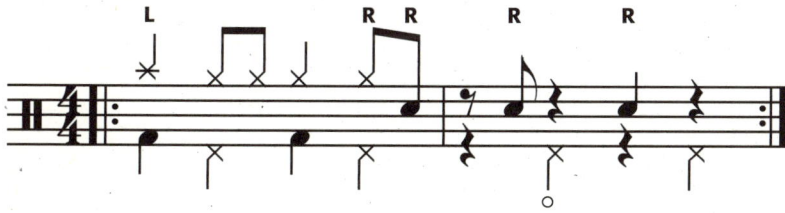

Now, let's try it again, but this time, we'll add an extra tom hit and a couple kick drum hits to the end of the fill.

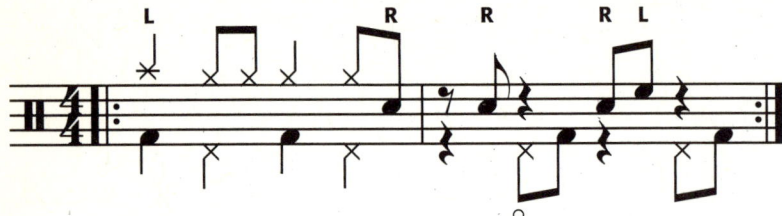

Finally, let's put it in context of the beat, and switch the wire brush to your left hand and the drumstick to your right hand immediately after hitting the crash on beat 1 at the end of the drum fill. This switch will take some practice, but be patient and stick with it!

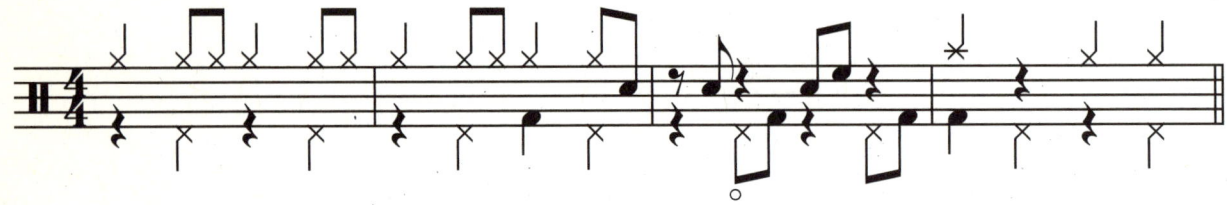

Stick Shot

A *stick shot* is played by placing the tip of one drumstick on the head of the snare drum while simultaneously hitting the shaft of the stick with the shaft of your other drumstick. The resulting sound is a loud, accented, woody crack.

When notated, a stick click looks like this:

"In Walked Bud" (ex. 3)
FROM THELONIOUS MONK'S *THE VERY BEST* (2005, SONG ORIGINALLY RECORDED IN 1947)

Art Blakey plays a drag immediately followed by a stick shot in this short drum fill. Play the drag by softly bouncing your right stick on the snare drumhead twice and then hitting the head with the left stick once on beat 1. Press the left drumstick into the drumhead rather than letting it bounce freely off the head like you normally would, and strike the left drumstick with the right drumstick on the "&" of beat 1. Then hit the snare with a normal stroke on the "&" of beat 2, followed by slightly-open hi-hats and the kick drum simultaneously on beat 3, and continue by playing a basic swing pattern on the slightly-open hi-hats.

Original transcription (2:12):

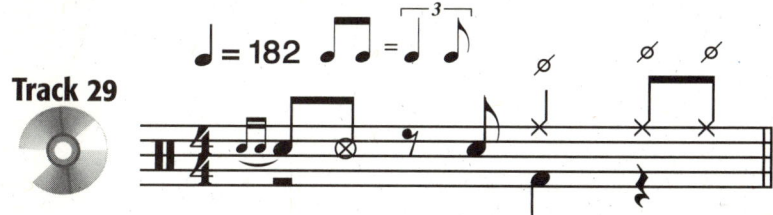

Track 29

Now, let's try playing the drum fill within the context of the song.

Track 30

"Chelsea Bridge"
FROM BUDDY RICH'S *THE BEST OF BUDDY RICH (PACIFIC JAZZ)* (1997, SONG ORIGINALLY RECORDED IN 1970)

Buddy Rich plays some smooth, well-placed drum fills in this section of the tune. Listen to how nicely he incorporates a roll into the third measure of this excerpt.

Original transcription (2:24):

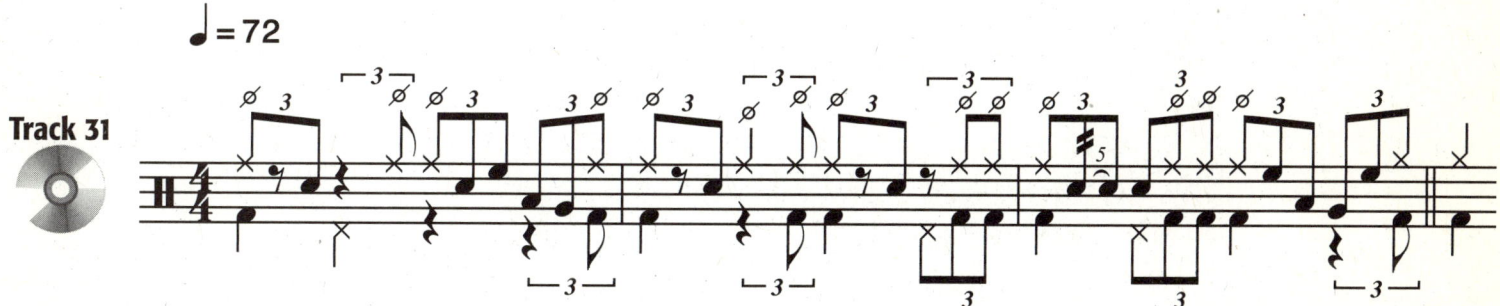

Track 31

Let's start by isolating and repeating the first measure of this excerpt. Start slowly at first, and gradually increase the tempo as you feel comfortable.

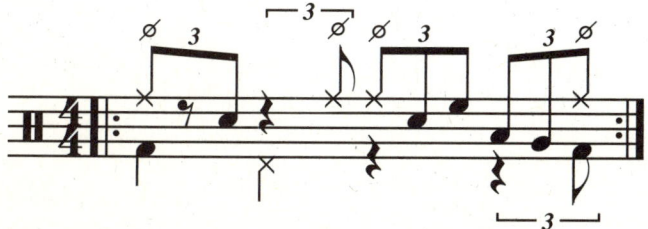

Next, let's isolate and repeat the second measure of the excerpt.

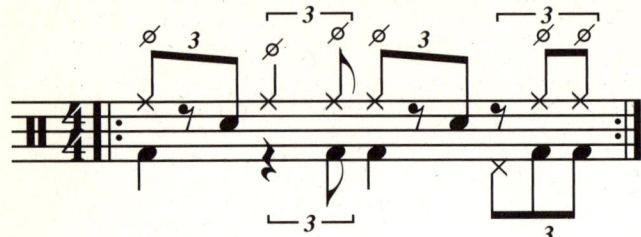

The fill incorporates a 5-stroke roll, which means the drum is struck five times throughout the course of the roll (RR–LL–R). The 5-stroke roll starts on the second note of the triplet that starts on beat 1 and ends on the last note of the triplet that starts on beat 1. Practice playing the 5-stroke roll within the beat by playing and repeating this exercise.

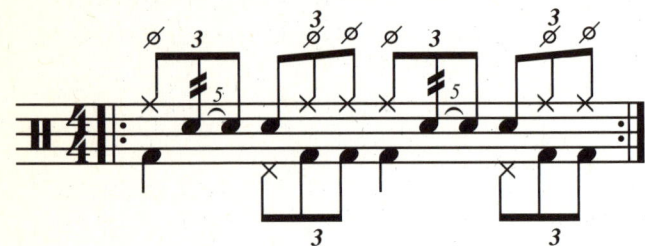

Now, let's isolate and repeat the entire third measure of the excerpt. Start slowly at first, and gradually increase the tempo as you feel comfortable.

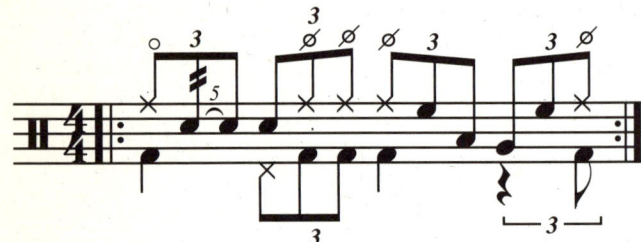

Finally, put it all together and play the fills just like Buddy Rich played them on the recording!

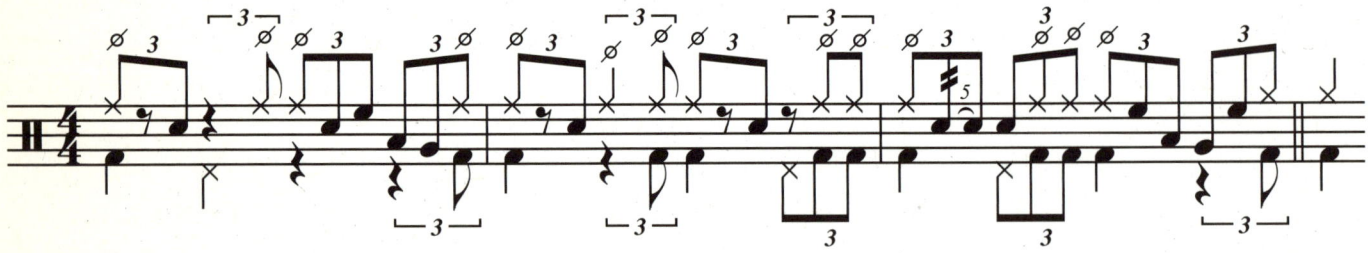

"In Walked Bud" (ex. 4)
FROM THELONIOUS MONK'S *THE VERY BEST* (2005, SONG ORIGINALLY RECORDED IN 1947)

Art Blakey incorporates a series of alternating stick shots and kick drum hits that are sandwiched in between a couple of drum rolls in this two-bar solo. Try playing the fill very slowly at first, and gradually increase the tempo as you feel comfortable.

Original transcription (1:24):

Track 32

Trading Fours

Trading fours describes when a group of two or more musicians each take turns playing a four-measure solo.

Buzz Strokes

A *buzz stroke* is a type of hit where the drumstick is pushed into the drumhead so it makes a buzzing sound. The buzz stroke essentially isolates what one drumstick plays in each stroke of a multiple bounce roll, also called a press roll or a buzz roll. When notated, a buzz stroke looks like this:

Sextuplets

A *sextuplet* is a group of six notes played in the time of four notes of the same value. Sextuplets are identified by a small numeral 6 over the note group. When notated, sextuplets look like this:

Eighth-Note Sextuplet   Sixteenth-Note Sextuplet

"Blues Walk"
FROM LOU DONALDSON'S *BLUES WALK* (1958)

In this excerpt, drummer Dave Bailey is trading fours with Ray Barretta on congas. This transcription focuses on Bailey's first three drum solos.

Original transcription (3:58–4:35):

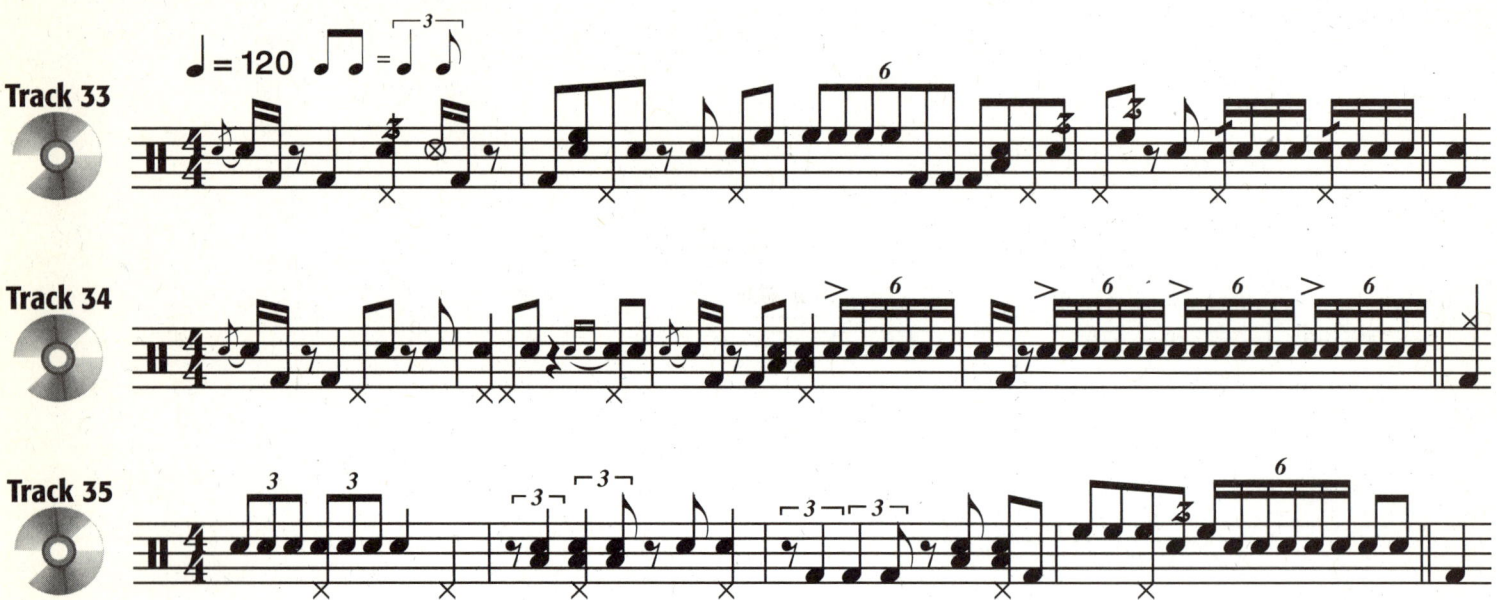

Let's start by isolating and repeating the first measure of Bailey's first solo. Play a flam on beat 1, a buzz stroke on beat 3, and a stick shot on beat 4, all on the snare, while playing the kick on the "&" of beats 1 and 4 and on beat 2, and while playing the hi-hat with your foot on beat 3.

Now, let's isolate and repeat the second measure of the first solo.

Next, let's isolate and repeat the third measure of the first solo. Bailey plays with some fancy footwork and ends the measure with a buzz stroke on the snare on the "&" of beat 4.

Finally, let's isolate and repeat the fourth measure of the first solo and the first measure of the conga solo. Bailey begins the last measure of his first solo with a buzz stroke on the high rack tom, and continues with sixteenth notes on the snare. The slashes that you see on beats 3 and 4 indicate that the stick should be bounced while playing that sixteenth note, similar to a double stroke roll, but with the double stroke only in your right hand.

Finally, let's play the entire first drum solo.

Now, let's isolate and repeat the first measure of Bailey's second solo.

Next, let's isolate and repeat the second measure of the second solo.

Now, let's isolate and repeat the third measure of the second solo. This measure ends with a sextuplet that begins on beat 4.

Finally, let's isolate and repeat the fourth measure of the second solo and the first measure of the second conga solo. This section of the solo features three consecutive sextuplets starting on beat 2. End the run of sextuplets by simultaneously hitting the ride and the kick, and then play the hi-hat with your foot on beats 2 and 4 while Barretta plays his four-measure solo.

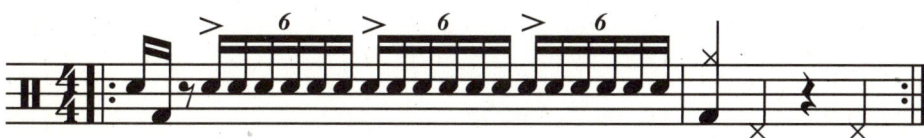

Finally, let's play the entire second drum solo.

Now, let's isolate and repeat the first two measures of the third drum solo.

Next, let's isolate and repeat the third measure of the third drum solo.

Now, let's focus on the last measure of the third drum solo, which contains a sextuplet on beat 3.

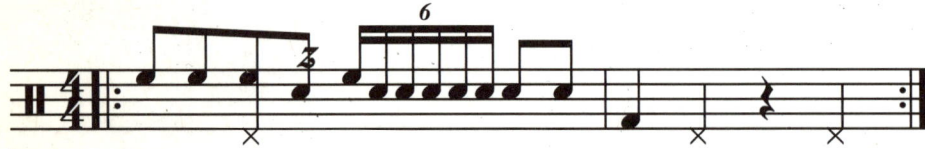

Finally, let's play the entire third drum solo.

"Money"
FROM PINK FLOYD'S *THE DARK SIDE OF THE MOON* (1973)

The Dark Side of the Moon is one of the most popular albums of all time. It was in the *Billboard* charts for an unprecedented 741 consecutive weeks and over 45 million copies of the album have been sold to date. Drummer Nick Mason plays along with Roger Waters's famous bass groove that is in $\frac{7}{4}$. That means there are seven beats to a measure, and the quarter note gets the count.

Original transcription (0:26):

Let's get comfortable with the $\frac{7}{4}$ time signature by playing this simplified version of Nick Mason's groove.

Add crash cymbal hits on beats 1 and 7, and an extra kick drum hit on the "ah" of beat 3, and you'll be playing the groove just like Nick Mason plays it on the recording!

"I Never Loved A Man (The Way I Love You)"
FROM ARETHA FRANKLIN'S *I NEVER LOVED A MAN THE WAY I LOVE YOU* (1967)

Drummer Gene Chrisman plays a wonderful groove in $\frac{3}{4}$ on this tune, sung by the Queen of Soul, Aretha Franklin, on her first single with Atlantic records. In this groove, there are three beats to each measure, and the quarter note gets the count.

Original transcription (1:05):

Let's start by playing a shuffle beat on the hi-hat, with hits on beats 1, 2, and 3, and on the "ah" of beats 1, 2, and 3. Also play the kick on beat 1, and the snare on beat 3. Go ahead and give it a try.

Next, let's play the same groove as in the previous exercise, but this time, we'll add another kick hit on the "ah" of beat 3.

Finally, play the same groove as in the previous exercise, but this time, raise your left foot off the hi-hat pedal on the "ah" of beat 2 and stomp it back down on the pedal on beat 3. Practice slowly at first and gradually increase the tempo as you feel comfortable.

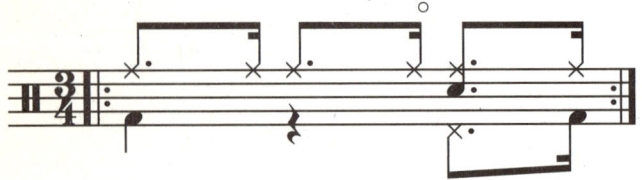

NEIL PEART

With his endless devotion to self-improvement and a true passion for excellence, Neil Peart has persistently elevated the art of drumming throughout his 30-plus years with Rush. Peart is known for his mastery of limb independence and for his ability to play musically and fluently in any time signature. Peart has rightfully earned an unparalleled level of respect among musicians and fans, and any drummer can benefit immensely by studying and learning from this true master of the drums.

"The Trees"
FROM RUSH'S *HEMISPHERES* (1978)

Neil Peart is one of the most respected and talented drummers to ever play the instrument, and he's inspired countless people to pick up the sticks and play the drums. Peart is revered for his ability to play well in any time signature. This excerpt and lesson features Neil Peart's $\frac{5}{4}$ groove on "The Trees."

Original transcription (2:53):

Let's start by playing quarter notes on the bell of the ride cymbal, the snare on beats 2 and 4, and the kick on beats 1 and 5.

Now, let's play the same groove as in the previous lesson, but this time, we'll add kick hits on the "&" of beats 2, 3, and 5.

Next, let's play quarter notes on the bell of the ride cymbal, the snare on beats 1, 2, and 4, and the kick on the "&" of beats 2 and 3, on beat 5, and on the "ah" of beat 5.

Finally, combine what we've learned in the previous lessons and play the $\frac{5}{4}$ groove just like Neil Peart plays it on the recording!

"I Hung My Head"
FROM STING'S *MERCURY FALLING* (1996)

Drummer Vinnie Colaiuta plays this $\frac{9}{8}$ groove so it flows almost effortlessly with a steady accent on every other hi-hat hit. Few drummers have mastered both the technical wizardry and the musical depth of Vinnie Colaiuta. He is without a doubt one of the greatest drummers who has ever lived.

Original transcription (2:20):

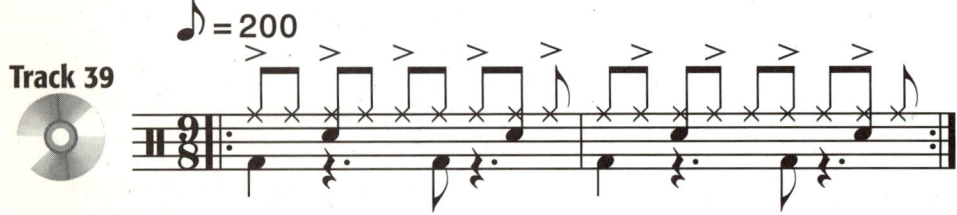

Let's start by playing this simplified groove in $\frac{4}{4}$.

Now, let's play the same beat, but this time we'll add one extra hi-hat hit at the end of the measure. You can count along with this as indicated on the example below.

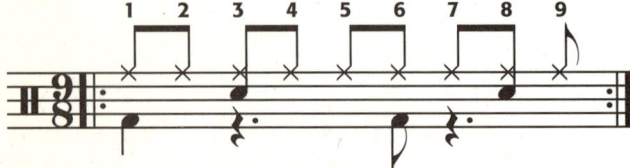

Next, alternate each hi-hat hit between accented and unaccented notes, starting with an accented hit on beat 1. Notice that in the first measure, you are playing accents on all the odd-numbered beats (beats 1, 3, 5, 7, and 9) and on the second measure, you are playing on all the even numbered beats (beats 2, 4, 6, and 8). This is a clever trick that makes time signatures like this flow very effortlessly. Start very slowly and increase the tempo as you feel comfortable. With a little practice, you'll be playing the groove nice and easy.

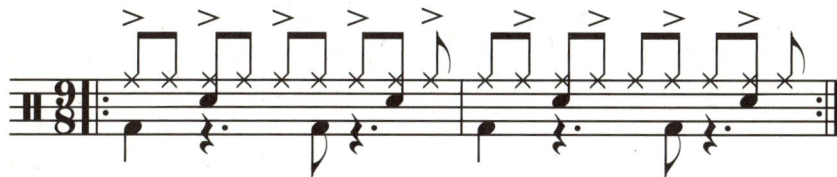

"Tom Sawyer"
FROM RUSH'S *MOVING PICTURES* (1981)

This is one of Rush's most famous songs, and it's one of the most inspirational tunes the band has ever released. Neil Peart plays a very interesting groove in ⅞ in this section of the tune that perfectly compliments Geddy Lee's synthesizer part.

Original transcription (1:37):

♪ = 175

Track 40

Let's start by getting familiar with the ⅞ time signature. There are seven beats to the measure, and the eighth note gets the count. Begin by playing sixteenth notes on the hi-hat with your right hand, the snare on beats 3 and 7, and the kick on beats 1, 2, and 6, and on the "&" of beat 4. It will take some practice to get used to playing in this time signature, so start slow, count out loud as you play, and gradually increase the tempo as you feel comfortable.

Now, let's play the same exact groove that we played in the previous lesson, but this time, we'll open the hi-hat on the "&" of beat 4 by lifting our foot off the hi-hat pedal, and stomping it back down again on beat 5. Go ahead and give it a try.

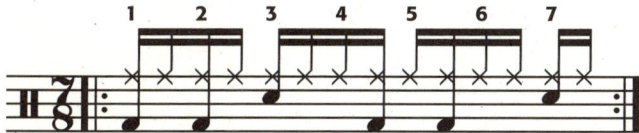

Next, let's play the same beat as in the previous exercise, except this time, well leave the hi-hat closed throughout and we'll move the kick hit from beat 6 to the "&" of beat 5.

Now, let's play the same exact groove that we played in the previous lesson, but this time, we'll open the hi-hat on the "&" of beats 4 and 5 by lifting our foot off the hi-hat pedal on the "&" of beat 4, stomping it back down again on beat 5, lifting it up again on the "&" of beat 5, and stomping it back down again on beat 6. Go ahead and give it a try.

Finally, let's put it all together and play the $\frac{7}{8}$ groove just like Neil Peart plays it on the recording!

Double Time

A *double-time* groove is a type of groove that contracts one measure into half of a measure. The most common and simplest application of a double-time groove is achieved by moving the snare drum backbeat from beats 2 and 4, to the "&" of beats 1, 2, 3, and 4. Note values and tempos are not changed when switching between regular-time and double-time grooves; only the *feel* of the groove changes.

"Me and Bobby McGee"
FROM JANIS JOPLIN'S *PEARL* (1971)

Janis Joplin, one of the greatest singers of all time, recorded this tune just a few days before her death on October 4, 1970, and the album that hosted this classic was released just four months later. Drummer Clark Pierson gives the song a boost at three minutes into the track by shifting his drum beat from playing in regular time to playing in double time.

Original transcription (2:56):

Let's begin with a simplified beat that will help us get comfortable with shifting from a regular-time groove to a double-time groove. In the first two measures, play eighth notes on the hi-hat, the kick on beats 1 and 3, and the snare on beats 2 and 4. Starting on measure three, play the kick on beats 1, 2, 3, and 4, and play the snare on the "&" of beats 1, 2, 3, and 4. Go ahead and give it a try.

Now, let's spice up the beat by adding a few crash hits, some extra hits on the snare and kick, and by switching from the hi-hat to the ride cymbal during the double-time section of this lesson. Start slowly and gradually increase the tempo as you feel comfortable.

Finally, add in a few more embellishments to make the beat authentic to what Clark Pierson played on the recording, and you'll be playing the groove just like it sounds on the album!

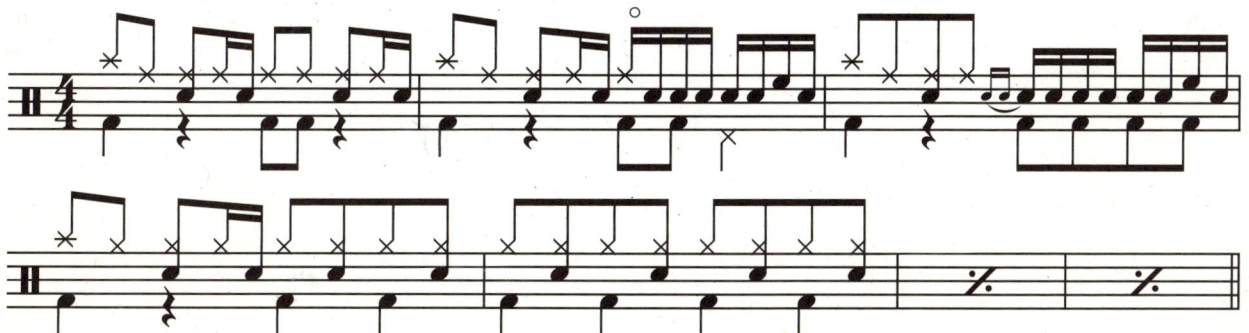

"Wherever I May Roam"
FROM METALLICA'S *METALLICA*, A.K.A. *THE BLACK ALBUM* (1991)

Powerhouse metal drummer Lars Ulrich shifts back and forth from regular time on the verses to half time on the choruses throughout this tune. We'll focus on one of these regular time to half time transitions in this excerpt and lesson.

Half Time

A *half-time* groove is a type of groove that expands one measure into two measures. The most common and simplest application of a half-time groove is achieved by moving the snare drum backbeat from beats 2 and 4, to beat 3. Note values and tempos are not changed when switching between regular-time and half-time grooves; only the *feel* of the groove changes.

Original transcription (2:10):

Track 42

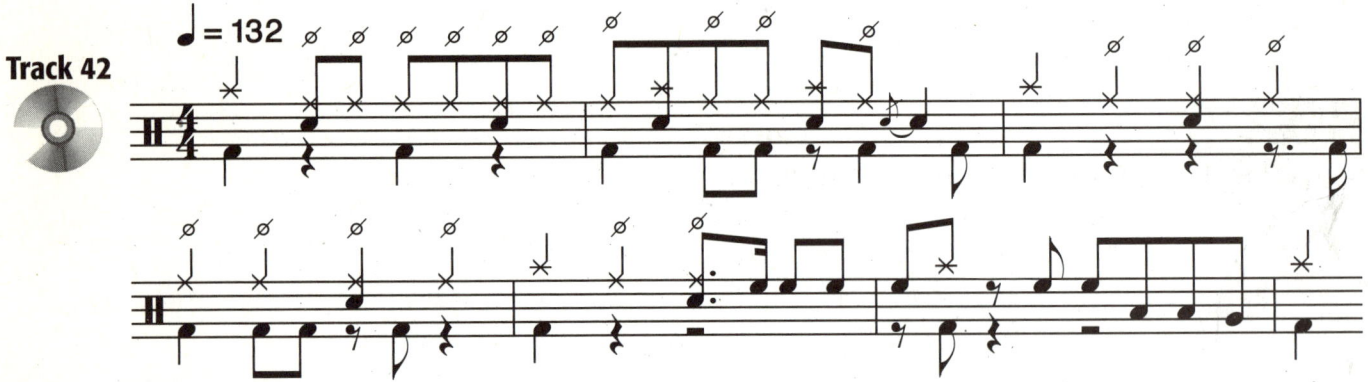

Let's begin by playing a simplified beat that starts in regular time and then transitions to half time. In the first two measures, play eighth notes on the hi-hat, the kick on beats 1 and 3, and the snare on beats 2 and 4. Starting on measure three, play quarter notes on the hi-hat, the kick on beat 1, and the snare on beat 3. Go ahead and give it a try!

Now, let's add some extra transition notes on the snare and kick in measure two, and spice up the half-time section with an extra kick hit on the "ah" of beat 4.

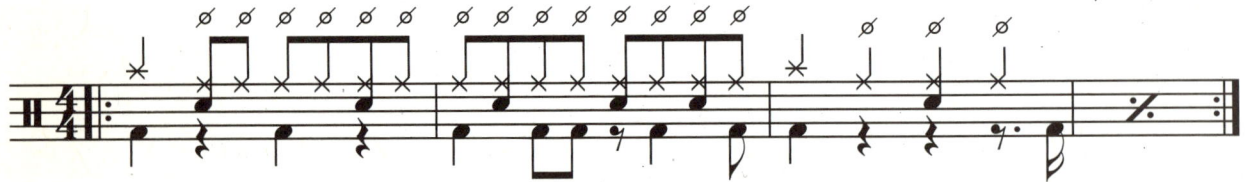

Finally, put it all together, and add some extra fills and embellishments as noted here. With a little practice, you'll be rocking this beat just like Lars Ulrich plays it on the recording!

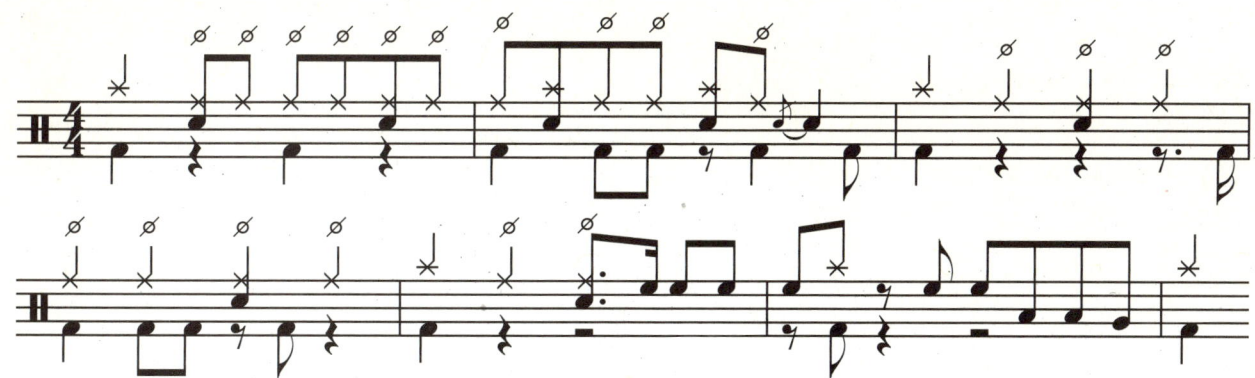

Metallica emerged in 1981, pioneering thrash metal in the United States at a time when glam was king, and they grew up to become metal's most famous and successful band. Lars Ulrich was firmly rooted behind the drumset, powering the band every step of the way. Lars has the ability to play hard and heavy whether he's playing his trademark lightening-fast double-kick thrash songs, or playing his slow epic grooves.

Ritardando

Ritardando is a musical term used to indicate that the tempo is gradually slowing down.

Accelerando

Accelerando is a musical term used to indicate that the tempo is gradually speeding up.

"Stand"
FROM BLUES TRAVELER'S *FOUR* (1994)

Drummer Brendan Hill guides the band through all sorts of tempo / time / meter manipulations on this tune. He switches from regular time to half time while giving the tempo a slight ritardando during his drum fill at 2:17 before leading the band through a very slow and steady accelerando over the next two minutes of the tune.

Track 43   Original transcription (2:10):

Let's start by playing a measure of regular-time at ♩ = 107 BPM, followed by the dramatic fill that ritardandos into a half-time groove at ♩ = 103 BPM.

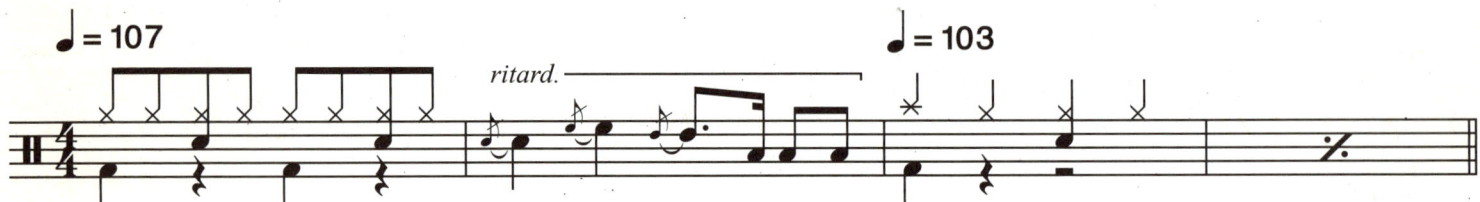

Now, let's practice transitioning from a slow half-time groove at ♩ = 103 BPM that accelerandos to a regular-time groove at ♩ = 125 BPM.

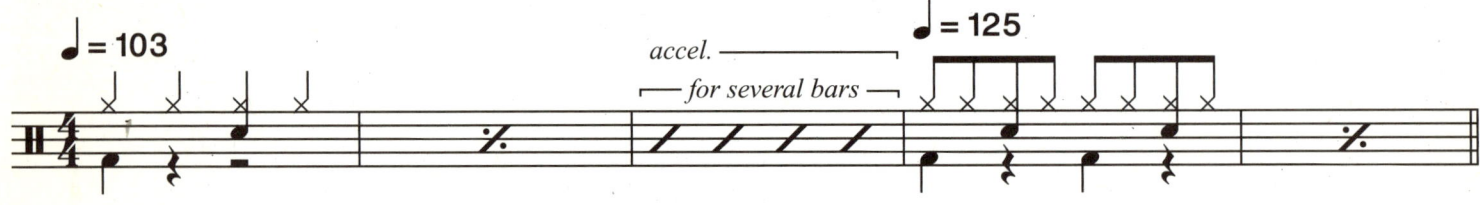

Finally, add in all the embellishments to make it sound like the recording, and really drag out the accelerando so it occurs over roughly two minutes of playing. Try making the tempo accelerate in a very steady, evenly paced manner.

Congratulations!

You have c o m p l e t e d **Level 3** of the
On the Beaten Path: Beginning Drumset Course. **You now have
all the tools you need** to play a
v a r i e t y of **musical styles,**

and to s t a r t   w o r k i n g   t h r o u g h
the other **On the Beaten Path**
series of books, like

*On the Beaten Path: The Drummer's Guide to Musical Styles
and the Legends Who Defined Them, On the Beaten Path: Metal,* **and**
On the Beaten Path: Progressive Rock,

to name a few. **And please,** if you're not already
playing in a **band,** it's time to find some m u s i c i a n s
to start playing with!
There's no greater feeling than **playing the drums**
and the music you love, so keep on drumming
On the Beaten Path!